MW01195697

Jazzed
ABOUT
Christmas

18 Christmas Songs in the Key of C Major for
Early Intermediate Piano Students

Music Mentor

JERALD SIMON

Learn how to play piano the FUN way!
The Apprentice Stage™ - The Maestro Stage™ - The Virtuoso Stage™

Music Motivation®
musicmotivation.com
Music that excites, entertains, and educates! ™

Music Motivation® books are designed to provide students with music instruction that will enable them to improve and increase their successes in the field of music. It is also intended to enhance appreciation and understanding of various styles of music from classical to jazz, blues, rock, popular, new age, hymns, and more. The author and publisher disclaim any liability or accountability for the misuse of this material as it was intended by the author.

I hope you enjoy **"Jazzed about Christmas!"** I am excited to have you play these 18 fun and easy to play, teacher and piano student friendly Christmas favorites.

The piano music is perfect for later beginner piano students and up, piano teachers, and anyone who wants to play. These are late beginner - early intermediate arrangements. You can listen to the music for the pieces from this book on my website, musicmotivation.com, and also on my YouTube channel - YouTube.com/jeraldsimon.

I hope you enjoy learning about this and all of my other music books! You can learn more at musicmotivation.com, http://essentialpianoexercises.com, and essentialpianolessons.com.

Your Music Mentor, Jerald Simon

This book is dedicated to my children - my daughter **Summer**, and my sons **Preston**, and **Matthew** - with a special thank you for my beautiful wife, **Suzanne (Zanny)**. I love you! I hope you all continually do your best in all you do! You can accomplish anything you set out to accomplish. Imagine the kind of world you would like to create and go about creating it. It is also for the many piano students enrolled in my **Essential Piano Exercises Course** (http://essentialpianoexercises.com).

I create these books from this series for all of you!

CONNECT with Jerald

https://www.musicmotivation.com/jeraldsimon
https://www.facebook.com/jeraldsimon/
https://www.youtube.com/jeraldsimon
https://www.linkedin.com/in/jeraldsimon/
https://www.pinterest.com/jeraldsimon/
https://twitter.com/jeraldsimon
https://www.instagram.com/jeraldsimon/
jeraldsimon@musicmotivation.com

CONTACT Music Motivation®

Music Motivation®
Cool music that excites, entertains, and educates!

Music Motivation®
P.O. Box 910005
St. George, UT 84791-0005
https://www.musicmotivation.com/
https://www.facebook.com/musicmotivation
https://twitter.com/musicmotivation
info@musicmotivation.com

First Printing 2009 - Printed in the United States of America - 10 9 8 7 6 5 4 3 2 1 - Simon, Jerald - Music Motivation® - Jazzed about Christmas - $12.95 US/ $14.95 Canada - Paperback book - ISBN-13: 978-0-9790716-8-3; Music Motivation Cataloging: MM00001009

Music Motivation® is a registered ® trademark

Music Motivation® - https://www.musicmotivation.com

Welcome to "Jazzed about Christmas" by JERALD SIMON

Piano teachers, piano students, and parents of piano students continually search for fun and exciting piano music their students can't wait to play.

The search is over with Music Motivation® and the music composed by Jerald Simon!

Jerald Simon is a popular pianist, composer, author, and performer/motivational speaker, who composes fun piano music that piano students love playing and performing for family and friends. Simon is well known for his **COOL SONGS Series** (https://www.musicmotivation.com/coolsongs) which features over 200 of his fun, original piano music - most of which include accompaniment MP3 minus tracks to help piano students learn to play the piano the fun way. He is also well known for his **Essential Piano Exercises Series** (https://www.essentialpianoexercises.com/pdf/series), as well as his popular Music Motivation® website and company (https://www.musicmotivation.com/).

In "Jazzed about Christmas," Simon has arranged 18 well known and loved Christmas songs for early intermediate levels that range in style from contemporary, classical, and new age, to jazz, blues, rock and pop styles. You will enjoy playing and performing these Christmas favorites as you have never heard them performed like this before.

It is the hope of the author and publisher that each of these jazzed up Christmas arrangements will uplift, inspire, bring a smile to the performers and listeners.

I'd like to introduce myself and tell you more about myself and why I love composing fun music to help motivate teens and adults.

My name is Jerald Simon. First and foremost, I am a husband to my beautiful wife, Zanny (her name is Suzanne - but anyone who knows her calls her Zanny), and a father to my three wonderful children, Summer, Preston, and Matthew. They are wonderful, and everything I do is for them. God and family always comes first in my life!

I am the founder of **Music Motivation®** (musicmotivation.com), and the creator of the Cool Songs Series (musicmotivation.com/coolsongs), and the Essential Piano Exercises Series/Course (essentialpianoexercises.com). I teach weekly online group piano lessons to students all over the world (essentialpianolessons.com). I have a YouTube channel (youtube.com/jeraldsimon), and I love learning everything I can, and want to help myself and others do our best and live our best life.

This is my Purpose and Mission in life:

"My purpose and mission in life is to motivate myself and others through my music and writing, to help others find their purpose and mission in life, and to teach values that encourage everyone everywhere to do and be their best." – Jerald Simon

Be sure to check out Jerald's **BEST-SELLING** piano book series: **Essential Piano Exercises Every Piano Player Should Know.** There are currently four books in the series. Other books in this series will soon be available as well (e.g. **Essential Pop Piano Exercises Every Piano Player Should Know, Essential Rock Piano Exercises Every Piano Player Should Know, 100 Chord Progressions Every Piano Player Should Know, 100 Improvised Licks Every Piano Player Should Know,** and so forth).

The four books currently in the series are:

"100 Left Hand Patterns Every Piano Player Should Know," "Essential Piano Exercises Every Piano Player Should Know," "Essential Jazz Piano Exercises Every Piano Player Should Know," and **"Essential New Age Piano Exercises Every Piano Player Should Know."**

You can learn more about these books from the Essential Piano Exercises Series and learn more about the course which you can sign up for at <u>https://www.essentialpianoexercises.com/</u>. The Essential Piano Exercises Series teaches fun exercises through original music I have composed.

A message from Jerald to piano students and parents:

If you come to piano lessons each week and walk away only having learned about music notation, rhythm, and dots on a page, then I have failed as a Music Mentor. Life lessons are just as important, if not more important than music lessons. I would rather have you learn more about goal setting and achieving, character, dedication, and personal improvement. To have you learn to love music, appreciate it, and play it, is a wonderful byproduct you will have for the rest of your life - a talent that will enrich your life and the lives of others. To become a better musician is wonderful and important, but to become a better person is more important.

As a Music Mentor I want to mentor students to be the very best they can be. If you choose not to practice, you essentially choose not to improve. This is true in any area of life. Everyone has the same amount of time allotted to them. What you choose to do with your time, and where you spend your time, has little to do with the activities being done and more to do with the value attached to each activity.

I believe it's important to be well-rounded and have many diverse interests. I want students to enjoy music, to learn to be creative and understand how to express themselves musically - either by creating music of their own, or interpreting the music of others - by arranging and improvising well known music. In addition, I encourage students to play sports, dance, sing, draw, read, and develop all of their talents. I want them to be more than musicians, I want them to learn to become well-rounded individuals.

Above all, I want everyone to continually improve and do their best. I encourage everyone to set goals, dream big, and be the best they can be in whatever they choose to do. Life is full of wonderful choices. Choose the best out of life and learn as much as you can from everyone everywhere. I prefer being called a Music Mentor because I want to mentor others and help them to live their dreams.

Your life is your musical symphony. Make it a masterpiece!

Music Mentor
JERALD SIMON

Music Motivation® - https://www.musicmotivation.com

Learn about my three stages of music success from my **Music Mentorship Map** below -
The Apprentice Stage™, **The Maestro Stage™**, and **The Virtuoso Stage™**
https://www.essentialpianolessons.com

The *Music Motivation*® Mentorship Map (for piano students)
by Music Mentor™ Jerald Simon

Music Motivation®
musicmotivation.com

	Apprentice — for 1st & 2nd year students	Maestro — for 2nd - 4th year students	Virtuoso — for 3rd year students and above
Repertoire	**Music Motivation® Book(s)** What Every Pianist Should Know (Free PDF) Essential Piano Exercises (section 1) Cool Songs for Cool Kids (pre-primer level) Cool Songs for Cool Kids (primer level) Cool Songs for Cool Kids (book 1) The Pentascale Pop Star (books 1 and 2) Songs in Pentascale position: Classical, Jazz, Blues, Popular, Students Choice, Personal Composition (in pentascale position - 5 note piano solo) etc.	**Music Motivation® Book(s)** Essential Piano Exercises (section 2) An Introduction to Scales and Modes Cool Songs for Cool Kids (book 2) Cool Songs for Cool Kids (book 3) Variations on Mary Had a Little Lamb Twinkle Those Stars, Jazzed about Christmas, Jazzed about 4th of July Baroque, Romantic, Classical, Jazz, Blues, Popular, New Age, Student's Choice, Personal Composition.	**Music Motivation® Book(s)** Essential Piano Exercises (section 3) Cool Songs that ROCK! (books 1 & 2) Triumphant, Sea Fever, Sweet Melancholy, The Dawn of a New Age, Sweet Modality, Jazzed about Jazz, Jazzed about Classical Music, Jingle Those Bells, Cinematic Solos, Hymn Arranging Baroque, Romantic, Classical, Jazz, Blues, Popular, New Age, Contemporary, Broadway Show Tunes, Standards, Student's Choice, Personal Composition
Music Terminology	Piano (p), Forte (f) Mezzo Piano (mp) Mezzo Forte (mf) Pianissimo (pp) Fortissimo (ff) *Music Motivation® 1st Year Terminology*	Tempo Markings Dynamic Markings Parts of the Piano Styles and Genres of Music *Music Motivation® 2nd Year Terminology*	Pocket Music Dictionary (2 - 3 years) Harvard Dictionary of Music (4 + years) Parts/History of the Piano Music Composers (Weekly Biographies) *Music Motivation® 3rd Year Terminology*
Key Signatures	C, G, D, A, F, B♭, E♭ & A♭(Major) A, E, B, F♯, D, G, C & F (Minor) Begin learning all major key signatures	Circle of 5ths/Circle of 4ths All Major and Minor key signatures (Identify each key and name the sharps and flats)	Spiral of Fifths, Chord Progressions within Key Signatures. Modulating from one Key Signature to another.
Music Notation	Names and Positions of notes on the staff (both hands - Treble and Bass Clefs)	Names and Positions of notes above and below the staff (both hands)	History of Music Notation (the development of notation), Monks & Music, Gregorian Chants, Music changes over the years and how music has changed. Learn **Finale** and **Logic Pro** (notate your music)
Rhythms	Whole notes/rests (say it and play it - count out loud) Half notes/rests (say it and play it - count out loud) Quarter notes/rests (say it and play it - count out loud) Eighth notes/rests (say it and play it - count out loud)	Sixteenth notes/rests (say it and play it - count out loud) Thirty-second notes/rests (say it and play it - count out loud) Sixty-fourth notes/rests (say it and play it - count out loud)	One-hundred-twenty-eighth notes/rests For more on rhythm, I recommend: "Rhythmic Training"by Robert Starer and "Logical Approach to Rhythmic Notation" (books 1 & 2) by Phil Perkins
Intervals	1st, 2nd, 3rd, 4th, 5th, 6th, 7th, 8th, and 9th intervals (key of C, G, D, F, B♭, and E♭). Harmonic and Melodic intervals (key of C, G, D, A, E, and B)	All Perfect, Major, Minor, Augmented, and Diminished intervals (in every key) All Harmonic and Melodic intervals Explain the intervals used to create major, minor, diminished, and augmented chords?	9th, 11th, and 13th intervals Analyze music (Hymns and Classical) to identify intervals used in each measure. Identify/Name intervals used in chords.
Scales	All Major Pentascales (5 finger scale) All Minor Pentascales (5 finger scale) All Diminished Pentascales (5 finger scale) C Major Scale (1 octave) A min. Scale (1 oct.) (Do, Re, Mi, Fa, Sol, La, Ti, Do) (solfege) All Major and Natural Minor Scales - 1 octave	All Major Scales (Every Key 1 - 2 octaves) All Minor Scales (Every Key 1 - 2 octaves) (natural, harmonic, and melodic minor scales) (Do, Di, Re, Ri, Mi, Fa, Fi, Sol, Si, La, Li, Ti, Do) (solfege - chromatic)	All Major Scales (Every Key 3 - 5 Octaves) All Minor Scales (Every Key 3 - 5 Octaves) All Blues Scales (major and minor) Cultural Scales (25 + scales)
Modes	Ionian/Aeolian (C/A, G/E, D/B, A/F♯)	All Modes (I, D, P, L, M, A, L) All keys	Modulating with the Modes (Dorian to Dorian)
Chords	All Major Chords, All Minor Chords, All Diminished Chords, C Sus 2, C Sus 4, C+ (Aug.), C 6th, C minor 6th, C 7th, C Maj. 7th, C minor Major 7th, A min., A Sus 2, A Sus 4,	All Major, Minor, Diminished, Augmented, Sus 2, Sus 4, Sixth, Minor Sixth, Dominant 7th and Major 7th Chords	Review All Chords from 1st and 2nd year experiences All 7th, 9th, 11th, and 13th chords inversions and voicings.
Arpeggios	Same chords as above (1 - 2 octaves)	Same chords as above (3 - 4 octaves)	Same chords as above (4 + octaves)
Inversions	Same chords as above (1 - 2 octaves)	Same chords as above (3 - 4 octaves)	Same chords as above (4 + octaves)
Technique (other)	Schmitt Preparatory Exercises, (Hanon)	Wieck, Hanon, Bach (well tempered clavier)	Bertini-Germer, Czerny, I. Philipp
Sight Reading	Key of C Major and G Major	Key of C, G, D, A, E, F, B♭, E♭, A♭, D♭	All Key Signatures, Hymns, Classical
Ear Training	Major versus Minor sounds (chords/intervals)	C, D, E, F, G, A, B, and intervals	Key Signatures and Chords, Play w/ IPod
Music History	The origins of the Piano Forte	Baroque, Classical, Jazz, Blues	Students choice - All genres, Composers
Improvisation	Mary Had a Little Lamb, Twinkle, Twinkle...	Blues Pentascale, Barrelhouse Blues	Classical, New Age, Jazz, Blues, etc. Play w/ IPod
Composition	5 note melody (both hands - key of C and G)	One - Two Page Song (include key change)	Lyrical, Classical, New Age, Jazz, etc.

Welcome to Jazzed about Christmas. This book is designed for the beginner/early intermediate piano student. There are 18 well known and loved Christmas holiday favorites in this book. Every arrangement in this book is in the key of C to help the piano players learn and understand the concepts in the key of C before attempting them in other keys (which can easily be done by moving chromatically or up to the right in half steps). The word chromatic simply means to move up or down using half step (i.e. C to C sharp, D to D sharp etc.)

These first five pages (pages 5 - 9) teach the theory used in each arrangement. Music theory simply means understanding chords, scales, progressions, key signatures, patterns, etc., and knowing what to do with it and how to use it. Many musicians have learned music theory, but have never learned how to use it. Many use music theory, but don't know what it's called and can't describe what they're doing and how they're doing it. I want to teach you what to do with that knowledge and how to use it in your own playing. Lets get started! To begin, play the C major pentascale below - first with the right hand, then with the left hand, and finally both hands together. The word "penta" means five. This is a five note scale. The notes in the example below are: C, D, E, F, and G. When you play C, D, E, F, and G one after another, you are playing the first five notes from the C major scale.

For fun, when you've mastered the example above, try playing all major pentascales in every key - moving up chromatically in half steps to the right.

Below is the same example as the one above, but we are playing the five notes from the C major pentascale as intervals moving up and down. The word interval simply describes the distance between two notes. For example, C, played alone, is called a first; C and D played together is called a second, C and E played together is called a third, C and F played together is called a fourth, and C and G played together is called a fifth.

For fun, when you've mastered the example above, try playing the intervals in every key - moving up chromatically in half steps to the right.

 Music Motivation® - https://www.musicmotivation.com

Jazz musicians enjoy using 6th and 7th chords (they also enjoy 9th, 11th, and 13th chords, but we won't discuss them in this book). We'll start by learning the basic triads (three note chords) in the key of C. The chords follow a pattern (major, minor, minor, major, major, minor, diminished, major). This is the progression of all triads in every major key signature. Look at the progression in the key of C below.

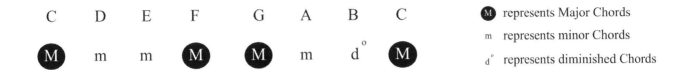

Some of the chords are major, some are minor, and one is a diminished chord. Play the triads found in the key of C major below. I tell students to "Say it and Play it!"™ That means to say the name of the chord, ie. C major, D minor, E minor, etc., when you play it. Try it.

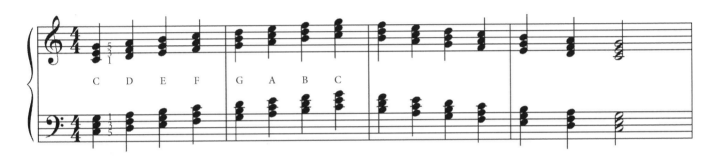

For fun, when you've mastered the example above, try playing it with the left hand, then the right hand and vice-versa. Play the progression of triads up and down the keyboard one octave, two, three, and even four octaves. You'll be surprised at how easy it is to do and you'll amaze yourself and others when you play this progression up and down the keyboard. Try it out.

Now that you've played the basic triads from the C major scale, lets talk about inversions. Every three note chord will have three positions because there are three notes. If we look at the C major chord, the three notes are: C, E, and G stacked on top of each and played at the same time. When C is on the bottom of the stack, the chord is in root position. Think of a tree with the roots at the bottom going down into the ground. If a strong wind uprooted the tree (and turned the tree upside down on it's head) the order of the notes would no longer be C, E, G, but E, G, and C. Since C is on the top, we call this a C major chord, but it is in first inversion. If we take the E off from the bottom and put it on top the order of the notes would be G, C, E. Since E is on the top, we call this a C major chord still, but it is in second inversion. Play the example below. Try playing the right hand, then the left hand, and then both hands together.

Now that you know how to play the basic C major chord, let's add one note at the end. The C major chord is C, E, and G. We're going to add an A to the end of it. Our chord will now be C, E, G, and A played together at the same time. This is called a C major sixth chord. Play the example below in root, first, second, and third inversions (since this chord has 4 notes, there is one more inversion than the three note chord). If you think this example is too difficult for you or your students to play, move on to the next example (but at least try to play it - you'll never know how easy it is unless you try - and the more you try it the easier it becomes). There are no four note chords in this book - I promise! Don't worry. This looks more frightening than it really is. Think happy thoughts! You're playing the same chord (C major sixth) every time. You're only changing the order of the notes. Play the C major sixth chord in root position, 1 •t, 2nd, and 3rd inversions. And as always, remember to "Say it and Play it!"™

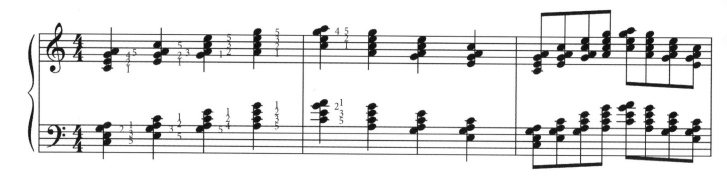

Now for the really fun part. Let's talk about how to use the C major sixth chord. There are several arrangements in this book that use the C major sixth chord played as a broken chord. When you play a broken chord, each individual note is played one at a time. A blocked chord, however, is where you play all the notes together at the same time. Play the example below with the left hand. The notes are C, E, G, and A played one after another. Jazz musicians will sometimes refer to this as a walking bass.

Turn to page 13 and take note of the similarities between the left hand in measure 10 of "Deck the Halls", and the example shown here. It's a broken sixth chord.

Now let's really jazz up this left hand pattern. Instead of playing the notes as quarter notes, we will play them as eighth notes. The progression is the same, except for one additional note. After you play C, E, G, and A, simply cross the index finger over the thumb to the B flat and then come back down. Play the example below with the left hand. The notes are C, E, G, A, and B flat played one after another going up and coming down. Jazz musicians also refer to this as a walking bass.

Pedal ad-lib throughout

If you feel adventurous, try this example in every key signature, moving up to the right in half steps each time. When you learn something in the key of C, always try it in every other key signature as well.

On this page, I've included several left hand patterns to be practiced before playing the Christmas arrangements. These left hand patterns are well known jazz patterns I have included and incorporated into each arrangement. Have fun with these. As with all exercises in this book, once you've played it in the key of C, always try to take it up chromatically, in half steps, through every key signature. These left hand patterns have been taken from my best-selling book, 100 Left Hand Patterns Every Piano Player Should Know.

This left hand pattern is used in "Jingle Bells" (on page 10) and also Deck the Halls (on page 14). It is a broken C6 chord. Try it with the F6 and G6 chords too.

This left hand pattern is used in "God Rest Ye Merry Gentlemen" (on page 16). It is a barrel house blues left hand pattern.

This left hand pattern is used in "Up On the House Top" (on page 13). It is a variation of a barrel house blues left hand pattern.

This left hand pattern is used in "Hark the Herald Angels Sing" (on pages 18 and 19).

This left hand pattern is used in "O Christmas Tree" (on pages 20 and 21).

This left hand pattern is used in "Good King Wenceslas" (on page 17).

This left hand pattern is used in "We Wish You a Merry Christmas" (on page 31).

This left hand pattern is used in "Deck the Halls" (on page 14).

Jingle Bells

Music by J. Pierpont
ARR. BY JERALD SIMON

Jazzy (♩ = c. 100 - 110)

Pedal ad-lib throughout

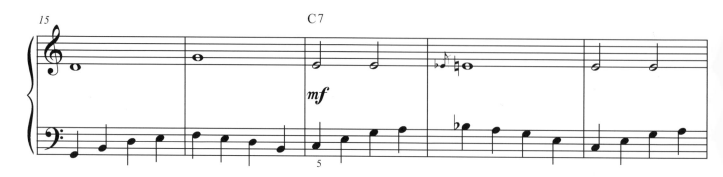

Jolly Old Saint Nicholas

Smooth and Cool (♩ = c. 108)

Traditional 19th Century American Carol
ARR. BY JERALD SIMON

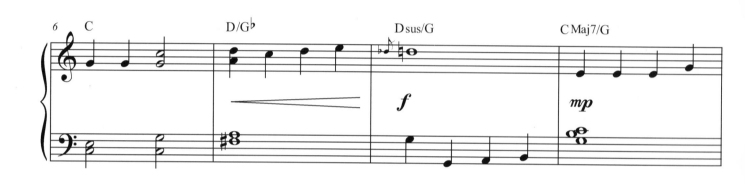

Pedal ad-lib throughout

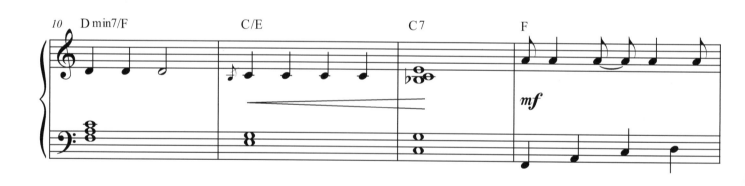

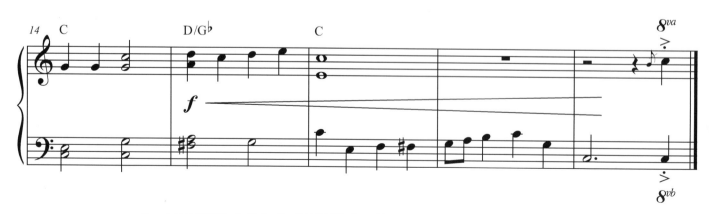

Up On the House Top

Music by B. R. Hanby
ARR. BY JERALD SIMON

Full of ENERGY (have FUN) (♩ = c. 120)

Pedal ad-lib throughout

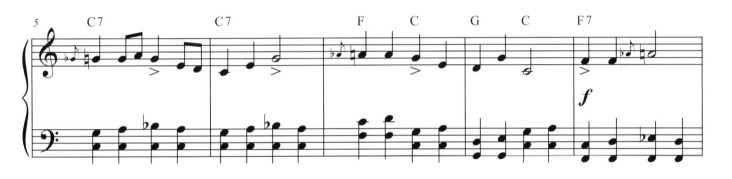

Deck the Halls

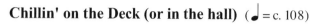

Old Welsh Air
ARR. BY JERALD SIMON

Chillin' on the Deck (or in the hall) (♩ = c. 108)

Pedal ad-lib throughout

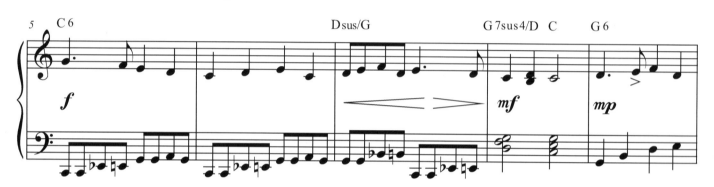

Joy to the World

Music by George Frideric Handel
ARR. BY JERALD SIMON

Smooth and Bright (M.M. ♩ = c. 120)

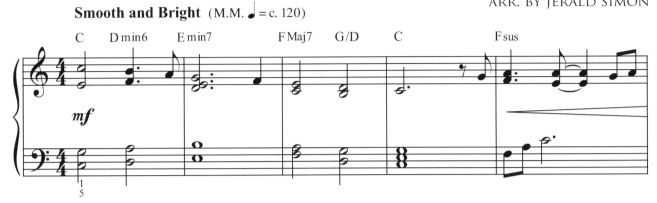

Pedal ad-lib throughout

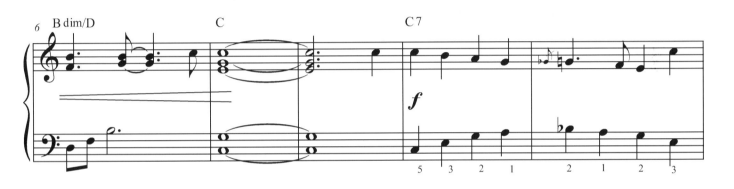

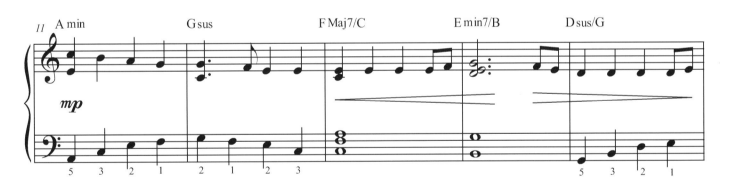

God Rest Ye Merry Gentlemen

English Carol
ARR. BY JERALD SIMON

Laid Back Blues Feel (M.M. ♩ = c. 100 - 115)

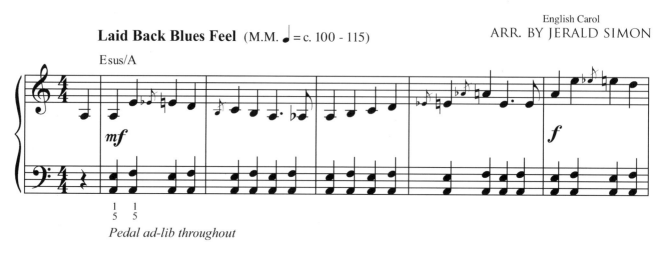

Pedal ad-lib throughout

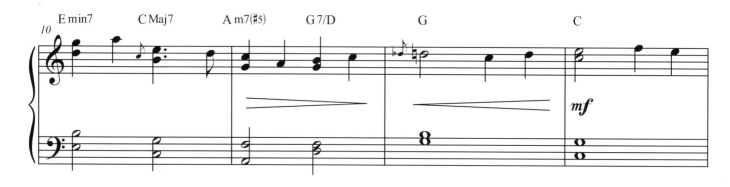

Good King Wenceslas

Chillin' - It's How the Good King's Feelin' (M.M. ♩ = c. 120)

Traditional
ARR. BY JERALD SIMON

17

Hark the Herald Angels Sing

Music by Felix mendelssohn 1840
ARR. BY JERALD SIMON

Upbeat (These Angels ROCK!) (M.M. ♩ = c. 120)

O Christmas Tree

Traditional German Carol
ARR. BY JERALD SIMON

Lively (M.M. ♩ = c. 120 - 140)

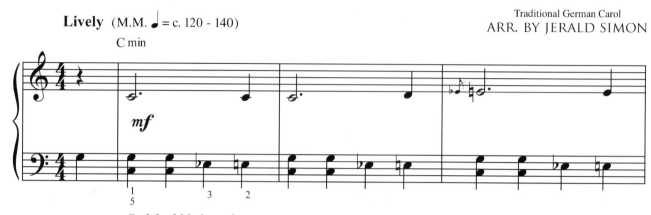

Pedal ad-lib throughout

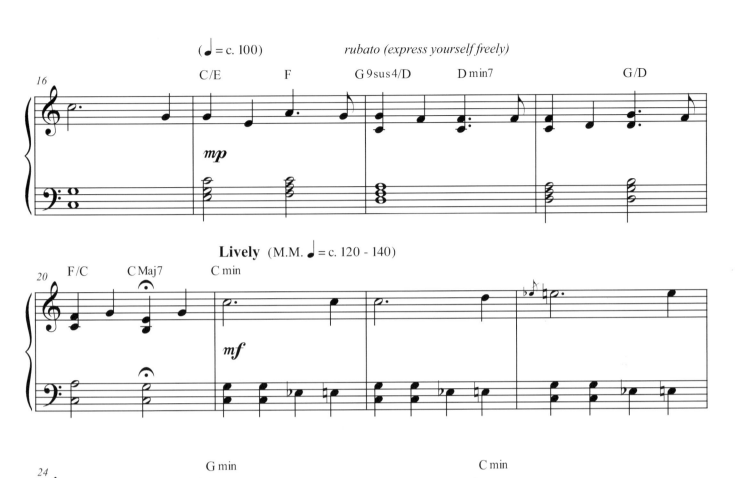

Angels We Have Heard on High

Old French Melody
ARR. BY JERALD SIMON

Sweetly and Gently (♩ = c. 96)

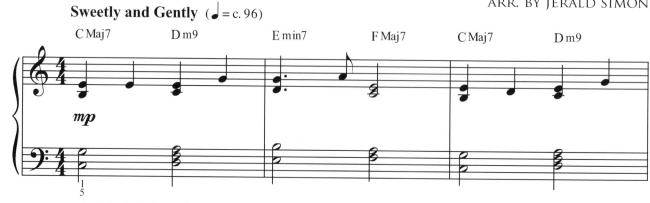

Pedal ad-lib throughout

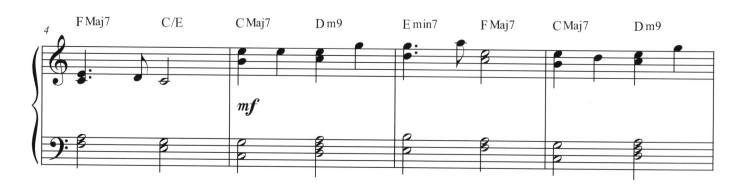

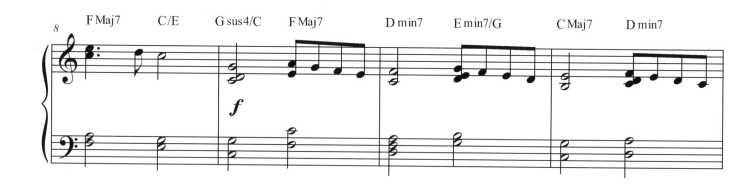

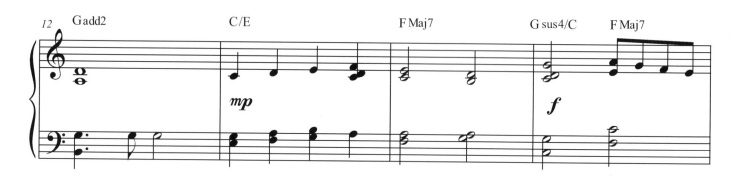

Silent Night

Franz X. Gruber 1818
ARR. BY JERALD SIMON

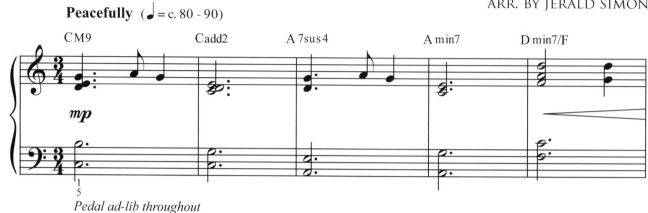

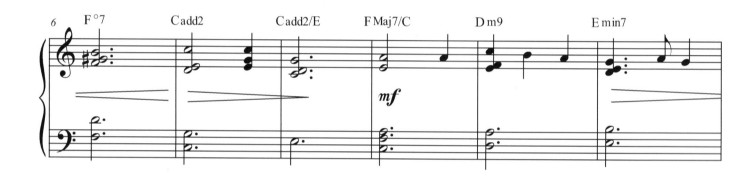

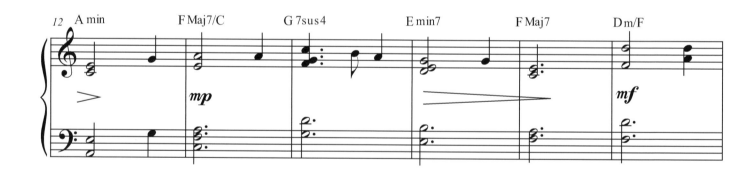

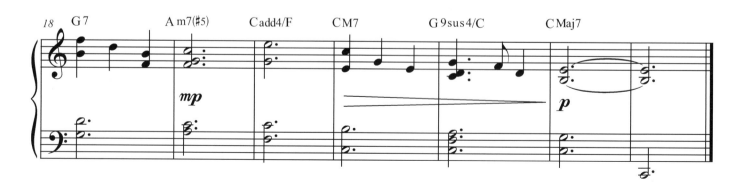

The First Noel

Traditional English Carol, ca. 17th century
ARR. BY JERALD SIMON

Easy and Laid Back (♩ = c. 80 - 92)

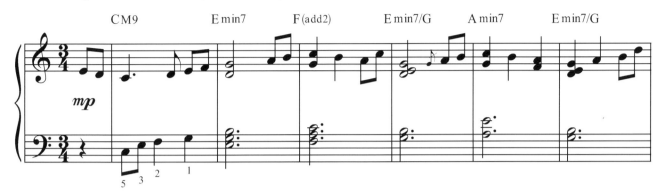

Pedal ad-lib throughout

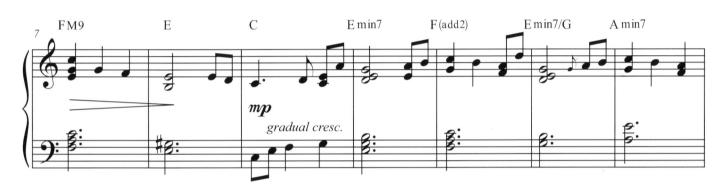

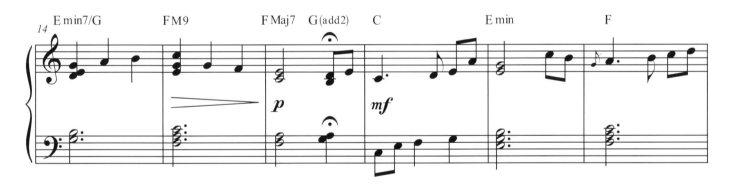

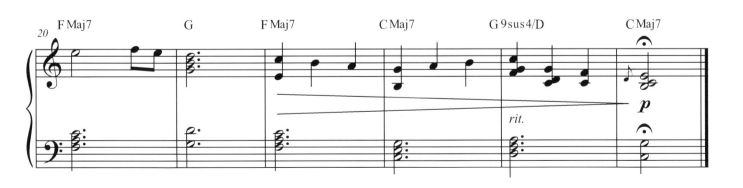

25

Bring a Torch, Jeannette, Isabella

17th Century French Provencial Carol
ARR. BY JERALD SIMON

With Somewhat of a Step (♩ = c. 120 - 140)

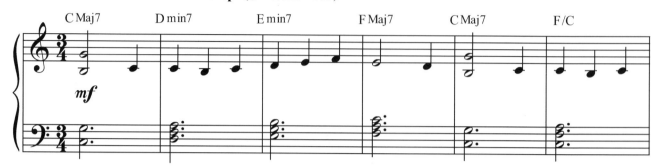

Pedal ad-lib throughout

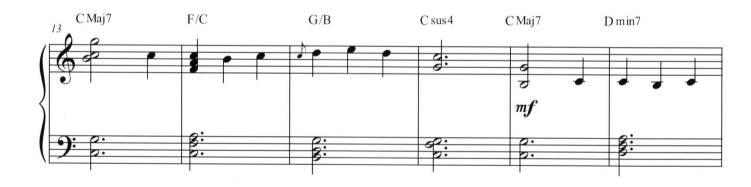

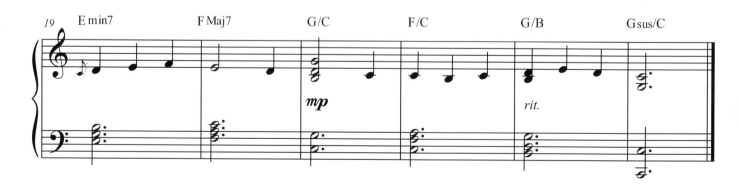

I Saw Three Ships

Traditional English
ARR. BY JERALD SIMON

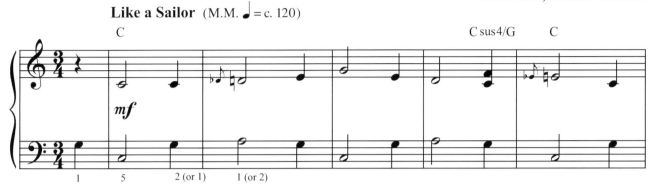

Like a Sailor (M.M. ♩ = c. 120)

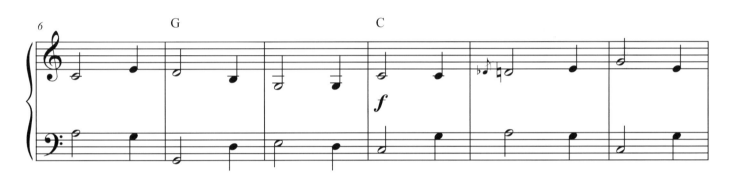

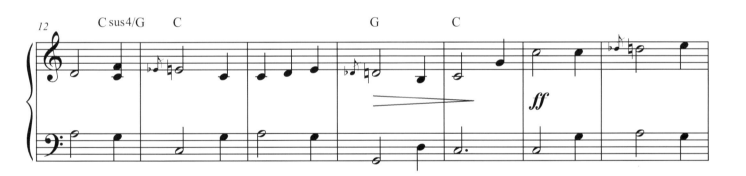

Still, Still, Still

Salzburg Melody, C. 1819
ARR. BY JERALD SIMON

Gently and Peacefully (♩ = c. 80 - 90)

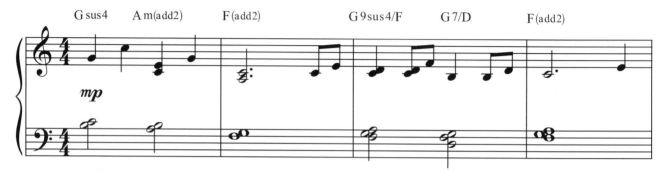

Pedal ad-lib throughout

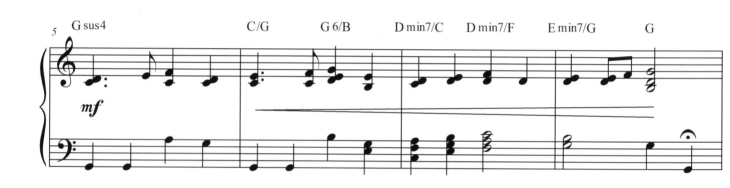

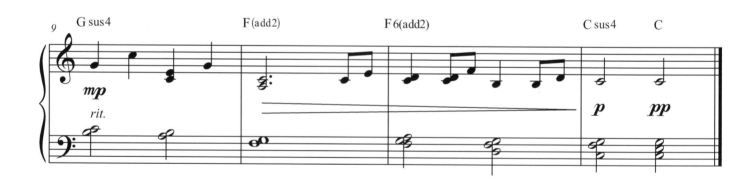

Dance of the Sugar Plum Fairy

Traditional English
ARR. BY JERALD SIMON

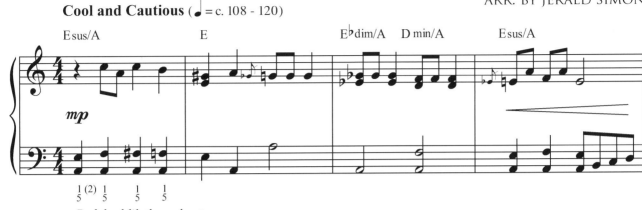

29

The Holly and the Ivy

Traditional English Carol
ARR. BY JERALD SIMON

We Wish You a Merry Christmas

Traditional English Carol
ARR. BY JERALD SIMON

Nice and Easy (♩ = c. 108)

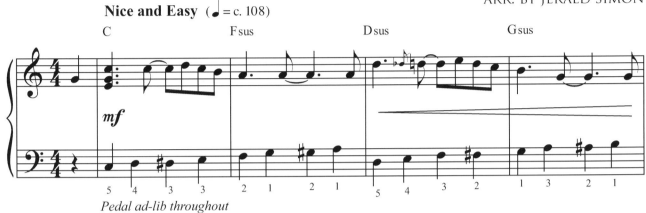

Pedal ad-lib throughout

A Few Additional New Age Music Books for Piano Teachers and Parents of Piano Students

If you enjoyed these Christmas arrangements, I think you will also enjoy working through contemporary classical/new age and cinematic sounding piano solos from my other books.

I teach about composing new age music in my Essential Piano Exercises Course (https://www. essentialpianoexercises.com/course). Within the course, I am uploading video lessons for every exercise and piano solo from each of the current books within the series. More books are being added to the series. I'd love to have you join the **Essential Piano Exercises Course**.

After you have had a chance to play through the various Christmas arrangements from this book, I'd love to have you film yourself playing one of these Christmas songs. You can share your video of you playing Christmas arrangements solo on social media, and I'd love to have you tag me in the video so I can see your great performance (@jeraldsimon). I always enjoy watching piano students perform music I have composed or arranges, and would love to see your progress!

Here is a URL link to a playlist on my YouTube channel that has music videos for every hymn arrangement from this book:

youtube.com/jeraldsimon

If you enjoyed these piano solos, I think you will enjoy the following additional books I have written.

Here are some titles to other new age music books and albums I have composed that you may enjoy:

Adventure Awaits - https://tinyurl.com/adventure-awaits-jerald-simon
Wintertide - https://tinyurl.com/wintertide-by-jerald-simon
Sweet Melancholy - https://tinyurl.com/sweet-melancholy
Sea Fever - https://tinyurl.com/sea-fever-by-Jerald-Simon
Triumphant - https://tinyurl.com/triumphant-by-jerald-simon
Castles in the Sky - https://tinyurl.com/castles-in-the-sky
Hymns of Exaltation - https://tinyurl.com/hymns-of-exaltation
Peace and Serenity - https://tinyurl.com/peace-and-serenity

Every so often, I try to release a new album/music book featuring meditation or relaxation music - all of which fall under the new age style of music. Most of these albums and books feature fully orchestrated pieces and not just piano solos. Some feature nature sounds, ocean waves, waterfalls, wind, crickets, or other soothing nature sounds and effects that have been combined with music. Many of these compositions are meditation/relaxation themed because they have been composed with the intention of helping the listener be comforted.

You can listen to my music on Spotify, Pandora, iTunes, Amazon, and of course, you can watch all of my music videos and additional piano lesson tutorials on my YouTube channel.

A Few Additional Ideas for Piano Teachers and Parents of Piano Students

You can visit this link to read the original blog post from which this presentation was created: (https://www.musicmotivation.com/blog/don-t-teach-music-theory-unless-you-teach-the-practical-application).

In the blog post, I talked specifically about 10 steps to begin teaching the practical application of music theory so students know their theory inside and out. I thought I would share the 10 steps here from the blog post:

Before any piano student plays their piece, I believe they should be able to do the following (this is what I try to have my students do with their music):

1. Tell their music teacher the key signature and time signature.

2. Identify all of the sharps or flats in the key signature.

3. Play all of the intervals created from the major key signature of the piece they are playing - this is more for piano students and possibly guitar students, as many instruments only allow one note at a time. If the student is younger or new to their instrument, they can play the intervals created from the pentascales or five note scales created from the first five notes of the major or minor scales.

4. Play through the major scale of the key signature of the piece at least 1-2 octaves up and down the piano (parallel and or contrary motion). If the student is younger or new to their instrument, as stated before, they can play the pentascales, or five note scales created from the first five notes of the major or minor scales.

5. Play what I refer to as the "Essential Piano Exercises" from each key signature. (In the blog post I show an example from the key of C major from my book "Essential Piano Exercises" - Intervals, Scales, and Chords in all Keys and in all Inversions - a 288 page book with all intervals, scales, and simple triads and 6th and 7th chords in all keys and inversions).

These are the other 5 steps:

Once a student can do the above five essential "getting started steps" in any given key signature (and many times I will do the following steps even if they can't do the above steps in every key signature), I then challenge them to do the following five essential "music theory application steps."

1. Once the student has learned and perfected the piece, ask him or her to take the song up half a step and down half a step. In the beginning, this is a good start. Later on, when they are better able to do so, have the student play the piece in any key signature. Start with simple pieces like "Mary Had a Little Lamb" and "Twinkle, Twinkle, Little Star." Have the students try playing these in all key signatures.

2. Ask the student to come up with at least 5-10 variations or arrangements of their piece.

3. Ask the student to compose 3 or 4 motifs (or single melodic line or phrase), and then put them together. This can be the beginning of creating a simple piece. I have students begin using scales and skipping notes here and there. We then have them take a simple pattern created from the notes of the major scale (1 2 3 4 5 6 7 8).

4. Ask the student to "Play a Rainbow." When I say this to students, I then begin to ask them to "play" anything. I may say: "Play me a shadow," "Play me a swing set," or "Play me a thunderstorm," "Play me a puddle, a rock, a tree, a meadow, a light, etc.". The sky is the limit. I first begin with tangible objects and eventually move on to intangible ideas and concepts: "Play me loneliness," "Play me disturbed, agitated, angered, humbled, pensive, etc.". Again, the sky is the limit. It is wonderful to see what students can create, even if they don't know all the rules of composition or terminology. Everyone has music within them.

5. I have students begin notating their music. I enjoy and prefer Finale, but that is because I have used it for so long and am familiar with it. There are many great programs available. After we have their music put down on paper, I then export the music from Finale as a midi file and open the midi file in Logic Pro. We then begin having them add additional instruments so they can create background tracks (this is how I create all of my weekly "**Cool Songs**" from my **COOL SONGS Series** (you can learn more about my COOL SONGS Series at this link: https://musicmotivation.com/coolsongs/). The students then have a PDF copy of their composition and an MP3 "minus track" to accompany them as they play. Talk about music motivation!

These are the books included in the COOL SONGS Series: https://musicmotivation.com/coolsongs/ -

The Apprentice Stage - The Maestro Stage - The Virtuoso Stage

COOL SONGS for COOL KIDS (Primer Level) by Jerald Simon
COOL SONGS for COOL KIDS (book 1) by Jerald Simon
COOL SONGS for COOL KIDS (book 2) by Jerald Simon
COOL SONGS for COOL KIDS (book 3) by Jerald Simon
COOL SONGS that ROCK! (book 1) by Jerald Simon
COOL SONGS that ROCK! (book 2) by Jerald Simon

Join the **Essential Piano Exercises Course** by Jerald Simon
https://www.essentialpianoexercises.com

Gain lifetime access to the PDF books listed below (which also includes video piano lesson tutorials where Jerald Simon demonstrates examples from the books and gives piano pointers, tips to try, and the practical application of music theory). Jerald demonstrates how to use the music theory to arrange and compose music of your own!

This course features pre-recorded video lessons so you can watch and learn how to play the piano at your convenience. You choose when and where you learn to play the piano.

Join the **Essential Piano Exercises Course** and receive the following PDF books along with access to the monthly video lesson taught by Jerald Simon for a one time payment of $199.95.

youtube.com/jeraldsimon

I upload new videos on Wednesdays, and Fridays on my YouTube channel, **youtube.com/jeraldsimon**. I have a few different playlists filled with great content for beginning - advanced piano students. The videos are geared for everyone from brand new piano students to music majors, professional pianists, and piano teachers of all skill levels.

There are three main playlists for my **free on-line piano lessons.** I do offer in person piano lessons, Zoom/FaceTime piano lessons, and step by step piano lesson packages you can purchase and watch at home (https://www.musicmotivation.com/pianolessons), but the ones listed below are FREE to everyone who subscribes to my YouTube channel:

1. **PIANO FUNdamentals** (emphasis on the word FUN!)
2. **5 Minute Piano Lessons with Jerald Simon** (sponsored by Music Motivation®)
3. **Theory Tip Tuesday Piano Lessons**

I frequently release new videos. Some are piano lessons, and others are filmed recordings of workshops, masterclasses, or concerts. I also have these additional types of videos on my YouTube channel:

a. **Meditation/Relaxation Music Composed by Jerald Simon**
b. **Hymn Arrangements by Jerald Simon**
c. **Motivational Messages by Jerald Simon**
d. **Motivational Poetry by Jerald Simon**
e. **Theory Tip Tuesday (FREE Weekly Piano Lesson Videos) by Jerald Simon**
f. **Cool Songs by Jerald Simon (musicmotivation.com/coolsongs)**
g. **Assemblies, Workshops, Firesides, and more...**

Let me know if you have a tutorial you'd like me to come out with to better help you learn the piano. I'm happy to help in any way I can and love hearing feedback from others about what they personally are looking for in piano lesson videos to help them learn to play the piano better. I primarily focus on music theory, improvisation/arranging, and composition. I refer to these as **THEORY THERAPY, INNOVATIVE IMPROVISATION, and CREATIVE COMPOSITION**.

I have also produced hundreds of COOL SONGS that teach students music theory the fun way. If you'd like to learn more about the COOL SONGS, that I composed to motivate my own piano students, or if you would like to purchase the COOL SONGS series featuring the music/books, simply visit musicmotivation.com/coolsongs to be taken to the page on my website that explains a little more about the COOL SONGS. You can also watch piano video tutorial lessons featuring 85 of the 200 + COOL SONGS (youtube.com/jeraldsimon). Let me know what you think. I'd love your feedback about the music. It helps me as I compose more COOL SONGS to motivate more piano students. I'm excited to have you watch my free video piano lessons on YouTube.com/jeraldsimon.

Learn more about
JERALD SIMON

Visit https://www.musicmotivation.com/jeraldsimon

"My purpose and mission in life is to motivate myself and others through my music and writing, to help others find their purpose and mission in life, and to teach values and encourage everyone everywhere to do and be their best." - Jerald Simon

First and foremost, Jerald is a husband to his beautiful wife, Zanny, and a father to his wonderful children. Jerald Simon is the founder of **Music Motivation®** (musicmotivation.com), a company he formed to provide music instruction through workshops, giving speeches and seminars, concerts and performances in the field of music and motivation. He is a composer, author, poet, and Music Mentor/piano teacher (primarily focusing his piano teaching on music theory, improvisation, composition, and arranging). Jerald loves spending time with his wife, Zanny, and their children. In addition, he loves music, teaching, speaking, performing, playing sports, exercising, reading, writing poetry and self help books, and gardening.

Jerald Simon is the founder of **Music Motivation®** and focuses on helping piano students and piano teachers learn music theory, improvisation, and composition. He refers to these areas as: **Theory Therapy™, Innovative Improvisation™, and Creative Composition™.** Simon is an author and composer and has written 30 music books featuring almost 300 original compositions, 15 albums (you can listen to Jerald's music on Pandora, Spotify, iTunes, Amazon, and all online music stations. Jerald's books and CDs are also available from Amazon, Wal-Mart.com, Barnes and Noble and all major retail outlets). He has published three motivational poetry books featuring over 400 original poems (poetrythatmotivates.com), and is the creator of the best-selling **Cool Songs Series** (musicmotivation.com/coolsongs), the best-selling **Essential Piano Exercises Series** (essentialpianoexercises.com) and Essential Piano Lessons for piano students (essentialpianolessons.com). He has also created **Essential Piano Teachers** for piano teachers (essentialpianoteachers.com). You can watch Jerald's videos on his YouTube channel at: youtube.com/jeraldsimon. Listen to Jerald's music on all streaming sites and his podcast, **Music, Motivation, and More – The Positivity Podcast** with Jerald Simon on all podcast platforms.

In 2008, Jerald began creating his Cool Songs to help teach music theory – the FUN way, by putting FUN back into theory FUNdamentals. Jerald has also filmed hundreds of piano lesson video tutorials on his YouTube page (youtube.com/jeraldsimon). In addition to music books and albums, he is the author/poet of **"The As If Principle"** (motivational poetry), and the books **"Perceptions, Parables, and Pointers," "Motivation in a Minute,"** and **"Who Are You?"**.

SPECIALTIES:

Composer, Author, Poet, Music Mentor, Piano Teacher (jazz, music theory, improvisation, composition, arranging, etc.), Motivational Speaker, and Life Coach. Visit **https://www.musicmotivation.com/**, to book Jerald as a speaker/performer. Visit **https://www.musicmotivation.com/** to print off FREE piano resources for piano teachers and piano students.

Book me to speak/perform for your group or for a concert or performance:

jeraldsimon@musicmotivation.com - **(801)644-0540** - https://www.musicmotivation.com/